Once Upon A New Orleanian

ONCE UPON A NEW ORLEANIAN

Michael Joseph

Once Upon A New Orleanian

Once Upon A New Orleanian
Michael Joseph

Copywrite©2011 / Michael Mangerchine

Published By Parables
March. 2019

All Rights Reserved. No part of this book may be reproduced or utilized in any form or by any means, electronic or mechanical, including photocopying, recording, or by any information storage and retrieval system, without permission in writing from the author.

    ISBN 978-1-945698-77-4
    Printed in the United States of America

Readers should be aware that Internet Web sites offered as citations and/or sources for further information may have been changed or disappeared between the time this was written and the time it is read.

Once Upon A New Orleanian

ONCE UPON A NEW ORLEANIAN

Michael Joseph

Once Upon A New Orleanian

Table Of Contents

The Dress Code	11
A Change of Heart	27
Piety and Inner Peace	42
System Lagniappe	57
More	76
Story Teller	91

Once Upon A New Orleanian

Prologue

Story is the unseen skeleton behind life's skin and the yarn through its fabric. And because it is in there somewhere, surely someone must be writing it.

But whom?

Did a well-intentioned sage begin writing the story long ago then bequeath the main idea and plot to a successor to continue writing it? Is this how the story of life has been passed down through time into our time and generations, from person to person, generation after generation?

Once Upon A New Orleanian

Who is weaving its plot and crafting the narrative? Is the story totally contained and maintained in the concrete, in the here-and-now and what-we-see? Are there abstracts behind what can be observed so as to make us wonder if there are other dimensions, even spiritual ones, to the story?

Perhaps the story of life is more than what merely meets the eye. Perhaps it does have a spiritual element as part of its abstract that can only be discovered and entered into by the soul that seeks another world, another dimension, a celestial city of sorts. And if this is true then how does one discover it?

Perhaps the few brief vignettes in this booklet will be serviceable for you in considering the possibility that there might be a spiritual abstract behind the concrete or physical, dimension of life. And if there is, due to its out-of-sight status, the stories in this booklet might help you to ponder what rocks to begin to look under in order to find it.

Here's hoping that you are on the path that will help you find out who indeed is the writer of the story of life. And if you've already been on the path and found out who the writer is I'll be pleased if, through these anecdotes, you'll be drawn more deeply into the story that is being written.

~ Michael Joseph

Note: Italicized terms in the stories are uniquely attached and/or deeply culturally meaningful to New Orleanians. An online search can usually explain the term.

Once Upon A New Orleanian

Inside are six brief stories

All are set in New Orleans contexts

Some were originally told
as stories by Jesus of Nazareth

The others relive some of His
encounters with people

———

There is a question
at the end of each story

Jesus of Nazareth originally
told this story. It is re-told here
in a New Orleans context

The Dress Code

Even when whites and blacks didn't bond easily Whitey Foster and LaMont Norskin were friends. They grew up in the same Gentilly neighborhood and hit it off from the start.

Both sets of parents were from the lower *bayou* parish and moved to New Orleans for jobs so neither knew anyone else in town at first. Their dads both worked for the Public Belt Railroad and years of shift-work together drew them close. They didn't talk much about racial matters though both were aware of what was going on. Their sons, Whitey and Lamont, were born only weeks apart and the families socialized often around crawfish boils, weekends at the fishing camp on Lake Pontchatrain, sports events, and Sunday church. That both families went to the same church only made the connection easier.

LaMont and Whitey went to the same religious-oriented grammar and high schools. Both played sports and hung out with the same crowds. Neither of them was overly attached to the religious beliefs that they were taught in school. The teachings were generally okay as far as they were concerned. But neither of them thought very deeply about the spiritual side of life.

As primary influencers their parents had rapidly gotten caught up in the New Orleans lifestyle, with some partying and gambling, and made time for family things though these usually centered around sporting events and social gatherings with others. And of course they went to church every weekend and special day. The boys would continue in these and many of the other colorful customs of the larger New Orleans culture.

Religion was, for many, just another one of the acceptable social norms for the New Orleanian.

As the boys grew they didn't neglect their mischievous sides. They noticed the girls and the girls noticed them too. Both were average in school and that about sums up their place in New Orleans culture. LaMont Norskin and Whitey Foster were average New Orleanian adolescents who were on their way to becoming common New Orleanians.

They would no doubt have three-to-five kids each, mortgage themselves on a home not too far from their parents while working lower middle-class jobs, experiment with abusive substances in the younger years, be married to one-two wives over the course of their lives, gamble a bit here and there, hunt, fish and golf some, enjoy their home football team, go to their kids activities and enjoy social events, food and drinks with a little cutting up, and hope all would turn out okay after a life full of Sunday visits to the place of worship.

    As young married men working to support families LaMont and Whitey stayed friends, shared other common friends, kept regular contact and did things together often. What made their bond so easy was that inquisitive, adventure-some, borderline risky spirit that they shared together from youth. Both loved to take a dare and give one back, fiercely compete, free-spirit in most things, rough-house, move fast, build and tear down, and trivialize and mock things that held no interest for them.

    By now the willingness to push the envelope a little in every aspect of life was a part of who each of them were individually, and who both of them were when together. And they loved feeding off of this quality in each of their natures even if it meant risky business with others, even other friends.

One such friend was Carmella Brucano. Carmella knew the boys in grade school, being in the same academic year since first grade. But they had few brushes together outside of school. By the high school years LaMont and Whitey had been to a few *king-cake* parties and sporting events where Carmella and a few other girls were and they formed a bond with her. Though they each went to all-boys and all-girls schools they hung out a lot, partied and caroused, jumped and jived, and the three confided about their love lives, school stuff, their sports involvements and the latest gossip floating around the New Orleans high school scene.

Their friendships were close enough to compel Carmella to dump a guy she was dating because Whitey and LaMont didn't get along with him. By the time of their senior prom their bond led them to pledge to have each of the other two in each of their wedding parties in the future.

Though Whitey and LaMont easily trivialized many things in life and were willing to play risky with all of their friends they were fiercely loyal and their bond with Carmella was to them a bond for life. In their minds they loved her like one loves a sister. And they would not miss the call to be in her wedding no matter the cost.

In time Carmella met the man of her dreams. He was a dashing, up and coming professional with that rare combination of rugged, raw manhood and a patient sensitivity that made him stand out. And Carmella was the light of his life. He was a prize in New Orleans and a lot of ladies who knew him felt like they had missed their chance. Carmella couldn't imagine how she had gotten so lucky as to land a man like Vincent. And she was additionally thrilled that LaMont and Whitey hit it off with him right away. He was glad to make room in the wedding party for the special friends of his bride. Carmella couldn't have been more pleased.

The week of Carmella's wedding was a typical week full of family, work, and the likes for LaMont and Whitey. Each week their wives agreed to give them a night off to hang out at the neighborhood bar. Often, though, they'd spat with their husbands about this, and over the childish riskiness that they often flirted with. Sometimes it got dangerous. But the boys never listened. That week they were in a particularly chipper mood.

They were in the frame of mind they were known to slide into when together, sipping beers and feeding off of one another's testosterone. They were happy for Carmella and wondered how they might make it a memorable day for her. Their good cheer and willingness to push the limits were kicking in and they were pleased with the special idea that they came up with. Carmella would love it.

Sal, the bartender, overheard their plan and warned them not to try it – he knew these guys. But as usual they just dismissed him.

Vincent Suprino came from a prominent Italian family in New Orleans. They had made it big in the grocery business and were well known in society circles. They were fun- loving locals for sure yet they had a certain dignity in social situations that was more notable when among casual friends and strangers. Their kind of dignity was especially practiced when it came to dressing nicely for the more formal occasions in life.

'Nicely' has its many interpretations when it comes to dress. And for the Suprino's and their large circle 'nicely' meant that propriety and good judgment would leave no stone unturned to be neatly and cleanly dressed in attire appropriate to the event. Nothing short of that could be tolerated.

The day of the wedding came. The ceremony was to the point and nicely conducted at the large historic church in the *French Quarter*. Carmella and Vincent bristled with joy as they walked to the limo that would whisk them away to the extravagant formal dinner and reception. Whitey and LaMont sent their families ahead to the reception. They had to "take care of something" first.

The reception center was downtown near the Mississippi River. Traffic was a challenge as there was a large convention in the city, but eventually guests were seated for the dinner. At the head table Carmella wondered where her two lifelong friends were. She had seen them at the wedding and their families were present. But where were they? She wanted them to each say a few words at the microphone. She was, in fact, holding up the reception and dinner until LaMont and Whitey took their seats.

      Little did she know that Vincent's first cousin was posted at the front door of the reception hall to ensure that all went well for the large event and that no mooching tourists would come in for a free party. Being from the suburbs of Atlanta he had never met LaMont and Whitey and didn't know who they were. Cousin Melvin was a massive man with whom dignity and honor was an obsession. His moma's roots were from rural Georgia and he had been reared a no-nonsense gentleman.

Once Upon A New Orleanian

At his side were his three brothers, additionally massive and with similar convictions. They were in hearty agreement with Vincent's father. He had noticed tourists in the halls of the large facility in their carnival costumes, yoking it up and having a good time. He had told them not to let any one in who looked like they didn't belong or who weren't properly attired. The day had been one big trial of their collective patience as more people showed up than expected, things were running late, the hallway noise was loud, parking was a nightmare and they were hot and hungry. They weren't in the mood for any funny stuff.

At the twenty-minute-late point the two rambunctious and very late New Orleanians bounded from a loud-sounding pickup truck which they left parked illegally on the extra-wide sidewalk outside the block-long outer glass wall of the

Convention Center. *Second line* music blasted from the truck's speakers as LaMont and Whitey danced their way through the glass front door and toward the door of the reception hall, just across a large hall from the glass street door.

Through the glass *the second line* music from the truck, seen outside through the long, high, top-to-bottom glass wall, could still be heard.

LaMont was decked out in full *Zulu Parade* attire. His light brown face was painted a charcoal black with white outline around his facial features. He had a coconut in one hand and a rubber-tipped spear in the other. Eighteen inch purple, yellow, and green feathers shot up from the back of his head while he clenched a large cigar in the side of his mouth. He grinned like Louie Armstrong and strutted like a peacock.

Whitey was fully dressed with the attire of a King Rex whose costume appeared to be painted on him. A purple cape with gold trim fell from his shoulders down his back to his calves. The glittered crown on his head was too small and he looked like Henry VIII without a kingdom. He had a green wand in his hand and make up on his face. He too, had a cigar in his mouth and in his hands were a chunk of *Mardi Gras beads* and a "*Rex, King of Carnival*" drinking cup. He beamed with glee and *second lined* beside his buddy.

Because the music inside the reception room overcame the commotion outside in the hall Carmella and Victor began the ceremony and the dinner unaware of the plight of her two friends. They, as well as the families of the two missing head-table guests, wondered where the men were.

As LaMont and Whitey danced their way upon cousin Melvin and his three brothers in the hallway just outside the door their parade was halted. The four large country boys in formal attire were not about to let the two capricious New Orleanians into the reception. They had never seen them before and besides they were not going to let them in dressed like that. For all they knew they were tourists wanting to get in on some extra fun.

Whitey and LaMont insisted on going in. They told Melvin and brothers that they were Carmella's best friends, and were to sit at the head table and say a few words. But it wasn't going to happen. Even if they were who they said they were they were not going in dressed like that. And no one came to the door to check for them and come to their aid. They could argue till they were blue in the face.

Whitey and Lamont were not going to be allowed in.

They had looked forward to this day for so long. They wanted to make it special for their special friend and to say to the large crowd how good a person Carmella was. They wanted to tell a story or two. They wanted their kids to hear them say things and experience how special friendships are.

After words didn't work the two ambitious friends made a move for the door. When they were blocked they started swinging. Each of them caught a few blows to the face and head that sent them to the ground. It wasn't over. A brawl ensued.

Whitey and LaMont awoke in separate hospital rooms that evening. Both had concussions. One had a broken nose and some stitches. The other a fractured jaw and a few more stitches.

They had missed the big event. Nothing in their power could undo the past. Their choices had been made which affected their outcomes.

Once Upon A New Orleanian

It was a choice that each of them made of their own accord.

Once Upon A New Orleanian

~

What assumptions were Lamont
and Whitey operating under?

Once Upon A New Orleanian

Once Upon A New Orleanian

Jesus of Nazareth originally
told this story. It is re-told here
in a New Orleans context

A Change of Heart

The Tranelles were an *Acadian* clan whose ancestors migrated to New Orleans in the 1820's. Their ancestors marketed fruit and vegetables in *the French Market* along the river. In time they ventured into corner grocery stores, floral shops, small clothing shops and tailoring, before finally opening what was to become a long-standing and very successful line of fine-dining restaurants.

They originally settled uptown along the Mississippi River near Maple St. where the current levee is today. A few floods later they moved to a modest shanty in the neighborhood that came to be known as the Irish Channel. After graduated successes in family businesses several generations later they moved into the upscale Garden District and became established socialites in New Orleans. Their offspring went to the finest New Orleans private schools and to prestigious universities around the country.

Francois Tranelle III had two daughters. Stephanie was the oldest and after college worked in the family businesses. She loved life with her parents, relatives and friends. Her future was set and Stephanie was too.

Anna was more of a skeptic. She was inquisitive, wandering and popular, with a sassy attitude to go along with her charm and good looks. Add to that she was smart, determined, opinionated and sure of herself. Stephanie constantly mothered her younger sister, often telling Anna that she wasn't listening. Anna would make temporary adjustments to get away from the heat only to go back to her former position. And by her late teen years Anna was absorbed with a growing discontent with the sheltered and penned-in life that she thought she had at home and everything that was New Orleans.

Her father was a decent and honorable man. He firmly believed that he shouldn't hide his long-term interests from his two daughters. He had told them of his significant resources and that he wanted them to eventually take over the family businesses. Stephanie was sold on the idea while Anna hid her true desires, not wanting to hurt her father's feelings. Her sights were set out there somewhere and her fervor to leave home was growing.

"New Orleans, New Orleans, blah-blah-blah; we think we're so cool and special because 'We're different,'" she would say to her sister. "'There's no other place like here?' Who the hell are we? Are we one step down from God or something? And nobody tell me I'm not listening!"

As Francois began to pick up how Anna felt about life and about staying home in New Orleans he decided to talk to his daughters about what was in the will for them if something were to happen to him and mother.

This, he hoped, would temper Anna's desire to leave home.

After going over the estate with them the girls were amazed. They knew they were in for a nice inheritance. But they weren't aware just how nice it was going to be.

Anna couldn't sleep for a week. Her spirit was in hyper-drive and she couldn't get over how much money she was in store for one day. For the next few weeks her thoughts would find shelter in the possibilities of what life could be like for her down the road. In a short time it became apparent to her that having that unsolicited information was feeding her growing passions. New Orleans with all of its nuances and customs was growing older by the day. There was life to be lived out there and she was missing out on it more than she could stand.

Anna was enthralled by the lure of the wild life. Her few adventures into it left her wanting more. Had she the time and resources she surely would heed its call. This line of thinking and her continued boredom with life in the family business was becoming a burden that she was no longer willing to bear.

Once in a while Anna was visited with the notion that maybe she was morally lacking in her outlook on life. No sooner would she wonder about that when she would quickly shake herself from it.

She didn't want to engage those kinds of thoughts.

Anna Trenelle was ready to cut loose and tap into her wild side and she just couldn't do that while at home. She had to go. And she knew how she was going to do it.

After supper one evening Anna prepared her father's favorite dessert and brought it to him. Following some small talk she laid out her wishes. Francois Trannelles was saddened at his daughters' request. He was not in total shock as he had seen the far-away look in her eyes before and had heard her say she wanted to leave.

Anna pleaded with her father for her share of the inheritance immediately. All the pent up passion for her to leave to pursue her wild dreams erupted in the dialogue with him. Of course she loved him and mother and appreciated their desire to give her a good life but it just couldn't be there, in New Orleans, in the family business. She wanted what was hers so she could launch out and apply all the good things they had taught her.

She declined to go into any detail about what she would do with her fortune. She yapped about starting a business and other things she thought her father wanted to hear. But secretly she was burning to cut loose and her intention was to make a straight line to Hollywood.

After trying to reason with his daughter Francois gave in to his soft side. He was afraid that he might be doing the wrong thing. But he wanted to believe in her. She was bright and ambitious. She could do anything she set her mind to do. And he couldn't bear to see her hurting so much. He decided to grant her request.

Within a few weeks Anna was on her way to Los Angeles. A friend in the film industry in New Orleans had hooked her up with a filmmaker with connections in Los Angeles. In a short time Anna was introduced to the Hollywood crowd and made friends quickly. Her outgoing, likeable style made her an easy fit. She didn't try to hide the fact that she was 'out there' to enjoy and be enjoyed.

And so it was. Anna rented a flat in the affluent part of town. After a few months she was welcomed in to the inner circle of one of the edgier groups of Hollywood jet setters and partiers. It wasn't long before Anna was off to exotic places with adventures around the world with the wild and the restless. She denied herself nothing and lived her days in wanton pleasure, spending money like she had an endless supply.

Many afternoons she awoke having to have friends recount the previous evening with her. The fun was captivating for awhile. As time went on it seemed like the adrenalin rush took longer to kick in. As her resources dwindled and the downtime lasted longer Anna noticed that there were moments when she felt lonely.

To relieve it she carelessly allowed herself to be lured by one of the rising Hollywood studs who had more ambition than he did sense. With him she had popularity and possibilities untold. After six months of living together he grew tired of her. She had no 'star power' and there were other women around who did. He dumped her like a hot potato. And to make matters worse she was stone cold broke.

Within a few weeks the few real friends she had were growing weary of her mooching off of them. One friend after another asked her to leave. Anna hocked the possessions she had to buy food and pay rent at motels until that ran out too. In this period she was growing increasingly lonely. Her friends didn't want her anymore. She had thought of calling her father. But she couldn't bear to tell him what she had done with her wealth.

In the three years since she left New Orleans she didn't once call her family. When they called her she talked briefly then ended their call quickly. She told them she'd prefer them not to visit her as she wanted to start a new life and she was traveling a lot. When it got heated she hung up on them. If they texted or emailed she tersely replied after awhile and asked them to please not contact her so often. Weeks grew into a month, then to several months before they would try again to call and get to see her. Anna had gotten what she had wanted. Now, with her life in shambles, she was longing for home.

For the first time in her life Anna's spirit was broken. She was alone and lonely and hung around the homeless shelters to survive.

Days became weeks and Anna had no contact with anyone she had previously known. She was down to a few changes of dirty clothes and a knapsack and slept where the wind blew her.

Her pride and fierce determination originally kept her from calling home. Now that pride was deflating. Deep desire, humility, and a sense of remorse began to sweep over her as she reflected on the loving life she once had and how she had brazenly treated her father because of her pride and selfishness.

"How could I ask for my inheritance while my parents are still alive?" she asked herself as she began to get in touch with her heart. "How could I be so disrespectful?"

She experienced how the down-and-out rely on leftovers and begging to subsist. When her thoughts went back to home she noted that her father's lowliest employees ate better than the fodder she could find. In time she longed just to go home and work in one of her father's restaurants as a janitor. Even they could afford to buy a warm fast food meal. She finally decided that this is what she would do.

In her newfound change of heart and sincere humility Anna Trenelles mustered the courage to hitchhike all the way home to New Orleans and beg her father's forgiveness. She would ask if she could just clean for him to get by. She didn't even deserve that.

Francois Tranelles was standing on the gallery of his massive Garden District home peering down the laissez-faire southern street, populated with large live-oak trees draped in thick, curly *Spanish moss*. Every evening for the past three years he found time to repeat this drill in the hope that one of those evenings he would see his long-lost Anna walking up the sidewalk toward home. This evening began like all the others.

After several deep sighs and a few short glances he noticed a worn, frail, woman headed toward his lavish home. She was in soiled clothing with a jagged knapsack over her hunched shoulders. Her hair was disgustingly wild and unkept. She looked down as she weakly but resolutely headed toward him.

Francois briefly looked away and then back toward the figure heading his way. Something seemed familiar but he had never seen a homeless person walking in his neighborhood. As Anna looked up she noticed her father's figure on *the gallery* of their home.

In her three years of wanton living on the wild side and her pitiful downfall in it, through the painful past few months of being destitute and hungry, her brave and strong spirit held in check her urges to breakdown and cry. But at the sight of her father gazing at her as she walked she could hold it in no longer.

Anna burst into heavy, convulsing sobs as she broke into a slow jog toward her father. She didn't have to run far.

Francois Tranelles III had realized that the woman he saw was his beloved Anna. In an instant he was moving as fast as he could toward her, arms spread as he moved, calling her name and weeping as he went, "My Anna! My Anna!"

Just before they met Anna cried out, "I'm sorry, father! I'm sorry! Please forgive me!" And she wept as they fell into each other's arms and held a long and tearful embrace. "If you'll just let me be one of your janitors in the business that's all I deserve for what I've done."

"Never, my Anna," he said as they sobbed together. "You will always have a special place in your family. You are my daughter and you always will be. You were gone and now you have returned. You will always be my Anna."

Once Upon A New Orleanian

~

Why Did Anna
change her mind?

Once Upon A New Orleanian

Jesus of Nazareth had many encounters with
ordinary people. This encounter is re-lived
in the form of a story set in a
New Orleans context

Piety and Inner Peace

By the age of five Eugene Petreaux knew that he was going to be clergy. And he never wavered in his desire. He lived and schooled uptown along the Mississippi River near *Audubon Park*. He was well-liked and had a cheerful and positive spirit. No one could imagine Eugene doing anything else. And after high school at St. John's he bolted for seminary and never looked back.

In seminary he ate up Holy Scripture. Above his other studies his interests in the Scriptures soared. He fed from them voraciously and they became the staple of his spiritual life into his ministry service and for the rest of his life.

Once Upon A New Orleanian

At the end of his studies and training he was ordained as 'Father Thomas' and eagerly embraced his first parish assignment. After twenty-five years of service that fostered his growth and maturity in service to His Lord he was sent to a parish near the lake.

Most of his new parishioners were like him, native New Orleanians, and he had a natural connection with them. Father Thomas was a priest who was out among his flock. He visited and served families and individuals in many of their needs, often serving among the poor in that particular part of his parish even though only a few of them ever came to the church. His favorite verse from Holy Scripture was John 20:21: "As the Father has sent Me, I also am sending you."

So he went.

Father Thomas would often go through life's struggles with his parishioners. There were those who sought him out for counseling and advice. And there were others who regularly served in parish functions but didn't want or feel the need for personal time with him. One such couple was the Belfonts.

Harold and Francine Belfont grew up along the river in the *Irish Channel*. They were World War II baby boomers and often referred to their life in the city then as "the good old days". Harold's moma grew up in the Channel with Francine's daddy in the 1920's and '30's. And both attended religious-based schools through high school.

Harold worked as a policeman growing through the ranks to sergeant and liked it at that rank. He served most of his career in the second district and the family lived in the Channel until retirement. Francine made sure the family went to church on Sunday. They rented half of a *shot-gun double house* and saved money when they could in the hopes of buying a house of their own one day.

The four children were born roughly two years apart at Sarah Mayo Hospital on Jackson Avenue. Katie, their fourth child had severe asthma the first few years. Her uncle Pootsie gave her shots on a weekly basis until the symptoms subsided. Katie's severe bouts with asthma and her sweet and outgoing disposition made her a favorite among her siblings, relatives, and friends.

Katie had a gift. She melted the walls that most folks construct around themselves. She was like the little Shirley Temple girl in the movies: outgoing, bright, affectionate, cheerful, talented, uninhibited, and saw good in everyone she encountered. She had a way of making most people feel good and one couldn't help but like her from the start. She was a ray of light wherever she went. And the young and the old alike were attracted to her.

She was in girl scouts and twirlers, liked to play hop-scotch and jax, and make-up stories with funny endings. Her older siblings took her for granted though they didn't mind her at all. She loved to do things for them even though they teased her sometimes.

"That's my family!" she would say. "They need their little sister." And she loved sitting on her daddy's lap and helping her momma in the kitchen.

In her third grade year Katie was preparing to be picked up by a friend and her moma one afternoon. As Francine pulled a brush through Katie's wavy brown hair she couldn't help but admire her daughter. That she was special could not be denied.

Francine gave her a warm hug as Katie headed for the door when

her ride arrived. She felt proud of
her little girl. But the warm feeling
was instantly evaporated by the
sound of screeching tires on the
narrow street outside and the horrible
screams of a woman and a little girl.
Instant terror gripped Francine as
she raced for the front door.

In the street, precious little
Katie lay dead, her life taken
instantly by a car whose driver didn't
see her until she gleefully skipped
out in front of him from between two
parked cars.

There had been no space to
park in front of the house so her ride
waited across the narrow one-way
uptown street. She yelled to Katie to
wait before crossing the street but
Katie was singing as she came
skipping out and a low-flying
helicopter was passing above them.

Katie didn't hear.

In a way the world ended for
Harold and Francine that day. Their
lives went on. Their other children

grew up and married. Grandchildren came and grew. But something died inside of each of them when Katie died. And each of them blamed themselves for it.

Neither spoke those words to anyone nor to each other but everyone close to them could see it.

And when family and friends pleaded with them to not blame themselves they only pretended to listen but did not hear. The inner voices of guilt and shame prevailed.

As the years passed Francine went back to work and Harold retired from the police force. He took another job to fill his days and they finally purchased a house out close to the lake.

They had always been Sunday's-only parishioners. But with the move they decided to step up their church involvement. The pain they had lived with for so long had for years stirred them to seek deeper spiritual answers. In a new parish they were going to finally do it. Their new parish priest was an uptown fellow by the name of Father Thomas.

Harold and Francine sprung into parish life. They joined committees during the week and attended daily *morning Mass*. When both officially retired they volunteered in social clubs, retreat planning, and finance decisions. They participated in the Mass and sang in the choir that formed. Both went to confession as many times per month as Father Thomas held them. They *prayed the rosary* each week and made many *novenas*. Each month they devoted a Mass to their Katie. In time they served with Father Thomas in the needs of the poor.

Thomas had heard what happened to Katie. But the Belfonts were silent about it. Over the years he worked with them many times. He noticed their somber devotion to the church and their devout participation. He also observed that they were reserved in happier circumstances when others were enjoying themselves. They were withdrawn from those kinds of interactions. They appeared to want to stay focused on the tasks when with others as if the tasks themselves were meant to give something back to them.

One day, going through the gospel of Mark in his devotions, the caring and spiritually sensitive parish priest stopped to reflect on the encounter Christ had with a young rich man. As he thought about the dialogue he sensed there was more for him to glean from it. So he prayerfully dissected the scene some more. As he continued to meditate on the passage of Scripture his thoughts went to the Belfonts.

Father Thomas had always had a burden for the Belfonts. But at that moment the burden was growing incrementally. A deep sadness overcame him as he sensed something about their deeper need that he hadn't before. He ended the time in Scripture with a time of praying for the family.

He committed the insights to His God and pledged to wait for God to lead him as to what to do with what he had just received.

Several months later Father Thomas sat in his study on a scorching New Orleans summer afternoon. The doorbell rang and upon opening the door he was pleased to see the Belfonts. They asked if he might have a few moments. He was pleasantly surprised at their seeking him out and was eager to visit with them.

After salutations and an awkward pause the Belfonts sat grimly in their seats. Thomas could see that something was troubling them. He waited. Francine began to sob and Harold held her hand.

The gracious priest felt a deep compassion for them.

Francine began, "Good Father Thomas, what must we do to inherit eternal life?" she said, looking down as she asked the question. Thomas instantly had a flashback to his time reflecting in Mark's gospel months before.

Francine explained that she and her husband had been trying for years to understand what was required for God to receive them into His heavenly kingdom for eternity. Harold added that they had worked hard to receive the *sacraments,* obey the ten commandments, and do things for others and for the church.

They said that something still seemed to be missing inside. All of their efforts to do right did not give them the inner assurance that they had gained eternal life. Thomas listened attentively.

After some length the hurting New Orleanians each repeated the question and waited for his reply.

"Harold and Francine, I have often thanked God that you are part of the life of the church. You have served hard and well. How could I have not noticed you in our midst? We've worked together many times. Your hearts to serve are strong hearts."

"But you are also poor and hurting in your spirits. You call me 'Good Father' but you know that only God is good. May I speak to your poor and hurting hearts?"

Both nodded their approval.

"You are so weighed down with guilt and shame for what happened to Katie. You blame yourselves and in that vein you come into the church. You have tried terribly hard to perform and to work to make up to God for what you've imagined that you have done, and do away with the awful guilt and shame that crushes you."

"You have tried to keep the commandments, observe the sacraments, and serve in the church all in the attempts to numb the pain from your guilt and shame. And yet your sorrows persist."

"Trying to earn your way into God's favor has been a terrible burden for you to bear. My heart aches for you."

Harold and Francine leaned forward, to the edge of their seats.

"Then what must we do **more**, as we're already doing all the good and right things we can see to do?" they asked, almost pleading.

"Each of you must go to God. Call on Him and admit that you have been carrying this burden most of your lives and ask Him to take it from you. He promises that He will in Matthew chapter eleven and verse twenty-eight. And open your heart to Him. He loves you. Receive His promise of forgiveness and eternal life through the sacrifice of Jesus Christ for you on the cross."

"What about our service in the church?" Francine asked.

"I love your service, but am sad to see you carry this totally unnecessary burden. Don't you want to be free from the guilt and shame that you serve under?" replied Thomas.

Harold and Francine did not answer.

"Doing good things, right performance and duty were not designed to take away the things that burden us. They are meant to be our glad responses to the Christ Who forgives us. Jesus Christ Alone can remove our burdens. That's why He died and rose again. Aren't you willing to let Him give you a new beginning of forgiveness and take your burdens of guilt and shame?"

With that the couple slowly rose and mumbled something softly.

They gave the priest sad looks then turned and walked out of the rectory door.

Once Upon A New Orleanian

~

Why were Harold and Francine sad
when they left Father Thomas?

Once Upon A New Orleanian

Jesus Christ had many encounters with ordinary people. This encounter is re-lived in the form of a story set in a New Orleans context.

System *Lagniappe*

Patrick O'Dowdy always assumed things would turn out alright for him. This was due in part to the culture he was surrounded with as well as his generic outlook on life.

He grew up in blue-collar Gentilly when every block could field its own kids ball team. There were so many kids whose families had moved into the newer Gentilly homes that finding something to do was a no-brainer.

The kids in school and in church were the ones with whom he biked and played ball and army with. They collected baseball cards, did pranks, and *went to the show*,

Pontchatrain Beach, and the lakefront. They romped and played together like most boys and girls did in those free-wheeling days gone by.

Patrick was not the easy going type. He was moderately successful in most things and known to lead the way a time or two. He wouldn't bend over backwards to help someone else and he was outgoing, fun-loving and confident in himself. He generally looked out for himself first and couldn't seem to listen to someone else's words for more than a few seconds before cutting the person off and running with the conversation himself.

Otherwise, like most kids, he was an avid participant in the many social and fun activities New Orleanians are known to enjoy.

Patrick had a small band of very close friends with whom he formed a tight-knit bond. They knew one another since youth or in several cases, since high school.

Once Upon A New Orleanian

And they shared some well-connected ties through which they looked out for themselves and for the rest who were in their circle.

They were mostly generational New Orleanians. Many of their ancestors had settled in *The Crescent City* after the great European migration in the late 1800's. The O'Dowdy's were second generation Irish whose ancestors moved to New Orleans to work in the expansion of the city in the early 1900's, and shortly after, to dig out the *Old Basin Canal*.

Patrick, and his close-knit band of buddies, could be named among the seventy-two percent of locals who grew up in Greater New Orleans and didn't leave the area.

He and his circle of friends knew someone who was related to, or was close friends with someone else they knew, or were related to, in virtually every walk of life.

Salesmen, administrators, city or parish employees, lawyers, teachers, office workers, politicians, and business owners among other professions were easily connected to someone in Patrick's inner circle or one of their relatives or friends.

And every native born daughter and son had extended family all over the city. When he had an old college buddy in from Texas for a month he couldn't believe how well connected everyone was. He kept remarking how "Everybody here knows everybody else!"

As he grew up Patrick understood that there were written rules and that there were 'pseudo' rules. The written rules in the *laissez-faire* culture were like the Ten Commandments he learned at school and church. Most of those were legal, cultural, and religious rules. And he took issue with a not a few of them that were disagreeable with some of his urges.

Not that he paid too much attention much of the time to the ones he would say that he agreed with. It boiled down to his presumption that if bending the 'rules' didn't appear to him to hurt someone else too badly then much of what was a 'rule' or the law was generally conveniently classified as situational ethics. (I.e., if the situation was an inconvenience to him then it wasn't unethical for him to break the rule, even if it happened to be against the law).

Others in his circle and beyond were governed by this view. And if a legal favor was needed to help one get out from under a 'situation' then often a phone call to someone followed by a little something under the table, or a promise of an IOU future favor would take care of the matter.

This is the way in which Patrick learned to conduct himself as a New Orleanian.

In this context he never worried if he would succeed in life. It would be more accurate to say that he assumed that with the right kind of maneuvering and having the friends that he had, and with their connections as well, he would do fairly well in life.

As mid-level municipal office manager in his mid-thirties he began to probe his circle of friends for other opportunities. He was on his second marriage. He had two children from his first wife and one on the way with his second. The nasty settlement obligations left him wanting for a greater financial margin to leave space in life for his toys and hobbies.

He was a fisherman and golfer. He also wanted to keep his season tickets to games for the state's college and pro football teams and continue to enjoy the lavish parties at home games. Alimony and child-support stole resources from these opportunities and he absolutely had to have them. These were core lifestyles and cherished customs in his machismo circle.

One in Patrick's inner ring was a friend of a political insider in a local parish. He knew of a position for someone with Patrick's experience and skill-set. Patrick had fished with him several times and that helped. Though the salary was a lateral professional move it was understood that certain linkages with particular well-positioned players would make for fringe benefits that were an unwritten part of the contract. This was part of the 'understanding'.

And after he asked some careful questions about supervision, reporting, record-keeping, and the press, Patrick took the job. He didn't disclose all of the fringe benefits to his wife.

In time Patrick began to enjoy and thrive in his new career with its

perks. He made new friends in the worlds of parish politics and business. Most of these new friends were casual acquaintances before or friends or relatives of his friends.
"Just like New Orleans," he laughed to himself in the golf lounge over drinks one afternoon.

After a few years he was approached by a strategist for a leading politician. He had been watching Patrick through a well-placed insider who had his eye out for talented and ambitious souls. He was aware of how 'business was done' by a man in Patrick's position and he offered Patrick the chance to apply his skills in a larger context and in places with 'bigger fish to fry'. No physical move would be required.

With Patrick's connections and skills he would simply move into a newer and nicer office and travel a little more. It became apparent to Patrick that he might make a few enemies from the work he would do in this new position. In a town where everyone knew everyone else this would be a tough choice. But he had made a few people dislike him in the past, especially in his last few years and it didn't hurt him.

Patrick was in.

In time his core circle shifted a little. A few of them became estranged to him. They were close enough to him to not blow the whistle but not so like him to go as far as he did to sell his soul to the system. In this new role he lacked for nothing and as long as no one was noticeably hurt, noticeably to him, that is, Patrick couldn't see what was wrong with it.

Over the next few years he was increasingly out of the loop with the more common of his old friends and relatives. He was an insider in a big machine that paid him handsomely at the expense of others. Patrick's opinion on that was that the political machine he operated in was making a difference in people's lives. If he had to operate under the table and gain from it in order for that to happen, so be it.

Of the guys in his original inner circle of home-grown New Orleanians the few who didn't care for the game Patrick was playing slowly fell out of his ever-secretive loop. Most of the boys played along and benefited as well.

Patrick O'Dowdy had never thought deeply about how hard work in itself often produces its own reward. He had never considered how faithful adherence to doing right in the 'little things' produced integrity in the larger things in life. He had become a product of the system he grew up in. Though many of the people in his life never descended to the level of underhanded profit-taking that he did, many of them exhibited the same mindsets on smaller scales in many areas of life.

Growing up, Patrick had adult role models who parked the wrong way on the street, blocked the sidewalk when parking in the driveway, threw bits of trash on the streets, ran unreported businesses, told 'white' lies, stretched the truth, denied facts, broke promises, and much, much more.

One early spring evening Patrick sat watching the local news while he paged through a fishing magazine. For the umpteenth time in the span of his adult life he listened to another reporter's investigation into yet another local public official who had leveraged his position illegally and for personal financial gain at the expense of the public.

For years he had relied on his soul-assurance that no current or former friend who knew of his doings over the span of his adult life would betray the Code of the New

Orleanian. That is: 'We have each other's backs while we wink at the rules and scratch each other's backs.'

There were times in the past, when seeing another TV report of a public financial scandal had stirred something in Patrick's heart. And for years he had no problem dismissing the inner questions that began to form. But on this particular spring evening the brevity and scope of all the deception began to weigh heavily on him. And for the first time in his life he didn't ignore the voice of his conscience in the matter.

As he thought about his life and the fact that he might easily be a primary subject in a public scandal he began to feel a lump in his throat as tears began to form in his eyes. He was watching a locally owned news channel that was owned by a wealthy and religious person who sometimes allowed local religious commercials aired on the channel.

Once Upon A New Orleanian

At the commercial break the sound of the soft music in the first commercial rode the sound-waves directly into his soul. They attached with the emotion that was bubbling inside of him, which then began to awaken tears in his eyes and a lump in his throat. As the music played a human voice spoke tender and kind words as if it were Jesus Christ speaking to the listener.

The words spoken were tender words of invitation to turn and receive forgiveness into a new life that only He could give because of His death on the cross for everyone. It continued for a moment and ended with a momentary, silent pause before moving onto a typical business commercial.

Something strange was going on and Patrick was gripped with the brevity of it.

It was dynamic, powerful, meaningful, and refreshing. It was as if an unspoken Voice was somehow speaking to his soul beyond the words coming from the television, a Voice from Some **One** - Some One there but not there. Like wind, seen yet unseen, definitely heard and all the while, not heard.

Something deep and spiritual and profound was happening. It was sudden and it was real, deep and personal. It cut deep and it was relevant. It was for him and to him. He could not deny it and he would not deny it.

Patrick O'Dowdy rose from his chair and walked resolutely out into the back yard away from anyone else. Without reservation he fell on his knees and quietly sobbed as he confessed and surrendered to the One Who spoke to him through the televised commercial moments earlier. A short while later he arose to his feet a new man.

On Monday morning he called his bosses and submitted his resignation, effective immediately.

He told those in authority over him that he wanted out and that he had no vendetta against them. They could relax.

After the calls he sat at his desk and checked the balances in his three savings accounts and two checking accounts. The total of all the funds was 2.63 million dollars and change. To the best of his recollection he estimated that 2.5 million of those dollars were obtained deceitfully, and/or, illegally. He longed to return those monies somehow but he had a wife and children to be concerned about.

The next day he confessed everything to his wife. While upset she was not surprised and in a way, relieved. She knew that things were going on that she didn't know about. And the way Patrick had evaded questions about some of the things he did and the money that he brought in was a giveaway.

Eileen was a good woman and a spiritual person in her own right. She had saved some of her own income from years working outside the home and knew that they would one day receive portions of inheritances from each of their parents. When Patrick informed her that he wanted to somehow pay back 2.5 million dollars to the parish her initial shock gave way to a warm admiration for her new husband. She could sense that something genuine, good, and real had happened between him and God. She had prayed for something like this to happen for years.

In faith they agreed that this is what they would do, as one, for the first time in a long time in their marriage. Both were confident that Patrick would eventually find employment again, a little more honorably this time around. Somehow, though costly, this felt good, and right.

The following week Patrick walked into the *parish* finance office.

He had arranged to meet with the parish chief-financial officer and had his personal attorney present. He produced a verifiable, anonymous certified bank check for $2.5 million dollars, payable to the parish, as a donation for the general fund. The signee on the check was his personal bank so no one knew they were from his personal funds.

He arranged for his bank manager to be called so that he could verify that the parish officer received it. Patrick informed the parish finance officer that this was an anonymous donation to the parish general fund.

Next, he visually recorded the moment and the check itself on his phone for verification in the small chance that anyone might say it never happened and sinister ones attempted to tamper with the funds before they ended up in the parish account.

He then called his bank manager again, this time asking her to speak <u>directly</u> with the parish officer to verify that she received the check. He then asked the parish officer to find the bank's phone number online, then call the bank manager back. He did this so that all would be certain that the transaction was indeed verified by the bank manager himself and not by an accomplice on the other line. The bank manager agreed that if the parish asked about where the funds originated he would inform them that they came from a well-meaning, wealthy citizen.

Patrick walked away knowing the deep and satisfying relief that accompanies the decision that helps one to be released from the crushing burdens of guilt and shame. He was a new man. His conscience was clear and his heart set free. He had experienced forgiveness from God through the Lord Jesus Christ for the first time in his life.

    He did not know what his new life would bring. But he knew deep inside that something happened to him. An undeniable new life was ahead, from the inside out.

~

What do you think of
Patrick's guilty reaction?

Once Upon A New Orleanian

Jesus of Nazareth originally
told this story. It is re-told here
in a New Orleans context

More

Jake Caprini was raised in
New Orleans back in 'the good old
days'.
Back then there were lots of
jobs, and *streetcars* and buses were
cheap, quick, and plentiful to
everywhere. Grocery stores were on
almost every corner of *the crescent
city* known for its square blocks.
Locally owned businesses abounded
uptown, downtown, and *back-uh-
town*. Manufacturing was thriving.
And it seemed as if everyone knew
everyone else's cousin, uncle or
parents.
As a youth Jake walked and
biked to most places. Things were
generally safe then, even for a city

known for its characters, charades and fun-loving people.

Into adult life he gambled a little, worked hard, drank a few beers, frequented Sunday church, generally stuck with he and his wife's families and a few friends, lived and partied modestly, put his kids through school, and saved some of his coins in the long-desired hope that he might retire and take it a little easier someday. But when it came to having the money to save for the retirement he desired there was hardly any *lagniappe*.

As the years came and went health issues required him to spend an increasing amount of time in various doctor's offices. And even if he could somehow afford the leisure retirement he had for so long hoped and worked for he was beginning to wonder if he would be healthy enough to enjoy it.

As he sat in the waiting room for yet another doctor visit he perused some of the magazines and other reading material on the table next to him. One skinny pamphlet caught his attention. It was titled: "The Bigger, Better Barn Builder". "What's dis about," he thought, "*Building a bawn*, always wanted to do dat." So he picked it up, leaned back, turned the page, and began to read:

"The Bigger, Better Barn Builder"

"From the deck behind his comfortable home in *Terrebone Parish* Patout Fourchon surveyed what his eyes could see of his sprawling and prosperous farmland. Like his Cajun forefathers before him he had worked hard to get where he was.

Five generations of hardworking Cajuns before him had amassed large amounts of land and possessions. As an only child he inherited down from his ancestors. And his holdings left him a nice nest egg. After careful investments in houses, land, and in the market he was not a poor man.

His portfolio looked good now and promising for the future. Through hard work and shrewd business dealings he had been able to buy bordering farmland all the way down to the *bayou*, not far from the Gulf, and expand his business operations. He employed a growing number of people, including a son-in-law he was grooming to manage his expanding operations.

Life was steady as she goes and full of things to do. He owned a lot of land that had multiplied in value. With the way things were going he had wondered for a few years now if he should sell some of his land and equipment to simplify his operations or if he should keep expanding the operations and retire to let his son-in-law run things while he sat back and enjoyed the fruits of his labors.

For a long time he wanted to build a camp a short-ways down the bayou near the Gulf and set up a shrimping business. He could do that and also spend more time hunting and fishing. This last option was attractive to him. After all, he had quite a few years of life left. He was robust and in good health. Why not let his assets produce even more for him to enjoy now and when he got older and have even more to leave to his kids and grandkids."

"Say what? Let's switch places, 'Bayou Ole Macdonald,'" thought Jake. "I'd retire right nah."

Jake continued reading.

"Patout didn't have to think on his decision any longer. He had worked hard, planned smart, decided wisely, and he deserved it. The sixty percent of arable land that he had in production brought in enough to produce a comfortable lifestyle. But he still had a lot of good soil just sitting there. And though his barns and sheds were large enough to store and process the crop that he currently harvested he wondered how much more storage space he'd need for the additional crop from harvesting the rest of the land. Why not just tear them down and build larger facilities? He could afford it. And this would ensure even more in retirement.

He had thought about this in the past. His wife, Moma Mignionne, wasn't convinced but he knew she would come around. He was sure of it. The next day he set his sights on his plan."

"Yeah you rite!" said Jake to himself. "See me? If I had half-uh what he had, I'd hang it up too."

He read on.

"Patout hired an architect and a contractor. He had them look at his barns and sheds, design and build new storage and processing buildings with state-of-the art equipment in their places and paid them handsomely. He had his son-in-law get the additional lands cleared, plowed and planted. And by the next harvest the work was done.

The first harvest was nothing short of spectacular, the new facilities were operational, morale was higher than the sky and Mama Mignionne was smiling. "Always a good 'ting," Patout mused.

While the new buildings were going up Patout began to scout out land down by the nearby Gulf for his camp. He hired his architect and contractors again to come up with his 'Mansion on the Bayou' as he began to refer to it. It was all he could think about. He had plenty of money, health, family, and plenty more money that would continue to come in for a long time. And now he had time to enjoy it all.

In what seemed to be a record short time his 'Mansion on the

Bayou' was done. It had nine bedrooms and five baths. The house had wireless for internet and twelve cable televisions. It was equipped with a Jacuzzi, hot tub, in-ground Olympic sized pool and a kiddie pool. It had a year round flower and vegetable garden, a private boat launch and dock, and a shed on the dock for ice and cleaning catch.

The dock could handle his three boats of various sizes and capabilities. The shed was for his jet skis and water skis equipment. In a giant shed behind the house he kept his many four-wheelers to race over the sprawling land and woods he owned behind his 'Mansion on the Bayou.'

As his land was teeming with game an additional spacious shed was built to process and skin the game that was to be hunted on his sprawling property surrounding the camp. It was equipped with large cold-storage containers for the game, catch, and other needs.

He and Moma Mignionne furnished the place in one giant shopping swoop during a trip over to New Orleans. They had determined that in one year from purchase they would have it all complete, furnished, outfitted and stocked. A year to the day later they would host the most lavish weekend *crawfish boil* southeast Louisiana had ever seen.

With everything in place and mission accomplished Patout Fourchon sat on his deck once again overlooking the new ultra-modern barns and storage facilities that were now stocked with massive amounts of recently harvested crop. Some was to be kept for storage and much being readied to be sold. Some was to be processed for immediate use for food for the family and the livestock.

It was a peaceful Louisiana evening sunset with a comfortable breeze crawling through the live oaks, magnolias, and azaleas that graced his property. In two days they would trek down to the completed and well-stocked 'Mansion on the Bayou' and launch his retirement with the party of a lifetime.

"Eat your heart out, Suc-cuh." Said Jake to himself. "Only in mah dreams."

Jake looked back at the pamphlet.

"As Patout sat with his feet propped up and hands cupped behind his head he couldn't contain the sensation of feeling very satisfied and proud of himself, his holdings, and his success. Careful planning, hard work and shrewd investing had paid off. Retirement was going to be nice, quite nice indeed.

'If Ah I must say so of myself,' thought Patout to himself,

'Patout have done quite well fuh himself. Wit 'lil educa-shawn, but a backbone and some wise 'tinkin and plannin', Ole Patout gonna make his pappy and his grand-pappy real proud, his *paran* too.'

Closing his satisfied eyes to savor the feeling Patout sensed an uneasiness beginning to creep into his consciousness. As the satisfying feeling gave way to the uneasiness a suppressed thought surfaced:

'What if da real meanin' of life is not in all dis? What if it has more to do wit giving to uh-thuh people 'dan wit havin' more than ah need? What if what really counts is how Ah've lived mah life fuh what comes **af-tuh** dis werld'?'

As these gnawing thoughts began to produce uncomfortable feelings Patout instinctively dismissed them out of hand. Why pay attention to such thoughts? There was too much too enjoy, too much life to live.

Anyway he cut it, he was a good man. Everyone knew that.

For a moment Patout recalled having this uneasy conversation with himself many times in the past. This one, like all the rest, ended with him dismissing any notions of mistaken priorities out of hand.

It was time to head to the kitchen for some *gumbo* and *boudin* that Moma Mignionne had prepared.

He loved her gumbo. And the boudin came from his own farm.

'Ahm goin-ta eat me somma dem food.' he chuckled to himself. 'Den ahm gonna fell me asleep watchin dem foootball game.

Mais yah, Cheh! Ah gah-run-tee.'

As he rose to his feet a revolting, lightening-quick pain bolted from his left arm up to his shoulder.

Impulsively grabbing his left shoulder he looked up from his feet and momentarily noticed his newly built bigger and better barns. In that fleeting second they suddenly didn't seem as important and satisfying as they had moments ago.

In the next instant another crushing jolt of sharp, halting pain from his left arm took a lightening quick u-turn at his shoulder and struck his heart. Though he had long thought he was a healthy man the years of stress, worry, bad diet, drivenness and more had taken their toll. The unknown condition inside of Patout had reared its ugly head in one dreadful, awful expression.

Patout fell dead on the deck."

Jake Caprini sat stunned in the waiting room.

"What?!? What kind of sickko writes a story like dis?" he shot back at the pamphlet.

He looked down at the last paragraph in the pamphlet. It began like this:

"This is a modern version of a story that Jesus told in the New

Testament. To read it in the words of the Christ go to…"

But Jake didn't finish the last paragraph. His emotions were boiling and he looked up from reading.

"Must be somebody who wants to make people feel guilty,' He almost thought out loud. 'What's wrong wit wantin' to have nice things and enjoy life? Some people just ain't satisfied 'till everybody else is miserable, Ah guess."

Just then the door opened and the nurse called out,

"Mr. Caprini, come on back."

Once Upon A New Orleanian

~

Why doesn't Jake
like the story?

Once Upon A New Orleanian

Once Upon A New Orleanian

This recasts both an event that took place with Jesus of Nazareth and a story that He told in the situation. It is re-lived and re-told in a New Orleans context.

Story Teller

Joshua Edwards was born in New Orleans' lower ninth ward and raised in the era of racial segregation. Though his family understood what bias, prejudice, and injustice looked like, they, and many others, didn't come through it feeling that they were owed anything. They saw what was going on and they felt the effects from it. They just weren't scarred by it. In Joshua's life this was largely due to his parents.

Joseph and Marion Edwards were multigenerational African Americans in the ninth ward.

Joseph's people had migrated from northern Louisiana and scratched out a living selling fruits and vegetables, and from fishing and *crawfishing*. His primary occupation was carpentry, learning the trade as a teenager. He helped construct some of the shantys that folk in the ninth ward called home back in those days. He also repaired boats.

Marion's people kept an old corner grocery store with her help until she married.

Joseph and Marion were exceptional citizens who stood out in their integrity and their kindness. And even though they were fairly involved in the life of their local church they weren't known for the legalistic stuffiness that accompanied some of their brethren.

What was noticeable about them was the selfless love and humility that gave color and light to what they believed. They were held by a view on life that energized how they lived and treated others. And they raised their children to value a blend of simple moral standards, truth, kindness, goodness, consistent endeavor, and appropriate doses of tenderness.

They knew how to love and laugh, apply themselves, gently correct and self-correct, and process pain when the tragedies of life visited them.

This was the environment which Joshua grew up in.

He was the oldest of five sons and several sisters. His four brothers: James, Joses, Judas and Simon, as well as his sisters, made for a hearty home with plenty of life, work, interaction and challenge. With a meager income all pitched in with family chores and to help in the struggle to get by.

Joshua worked with his daddy in his carpentry work at an early age. And by his adolescent years Joshua was a fairly skilled craftsman. His moma taught the kids to read, write, a little arithmetic and regular Bible lessons at home. Joseph and Miriam did their best to get them as much schooling as was possible in those meager and socially challenging times.

    Neighbors noted that the Edwards family bonded together so well after a painful beginning. In her engagement to Joseph Marion was raped by a stranger and the ordeal left her pregnant with Joshua. When he learned of this Joseph thought to end the engagement but he loved Marion. With no witnesses Marion's account was not believed by some even though Marion had shown no inclination to be the type to be foolin' around. After an intense time on his knees Joseph decided to marry Marion quickly and privately before more rumors spread.

    Some suspected that Joseph had gotten Marion pregnant during the engagement. As these kinds of things weren't totally uncommon in all cultures across New Orleans, Joseph and Marion were by and large not ostracized, although there were a few who never could let go of the rumors.

Joseph was up to the task and loved Joshua as his own son and never thought that he was a mistake.

Joshua was unique among most children. He was a typical New Orleans ninth ward boy in many respects. He explored and romped with other kids. But he had a noticeable goodness to him that stood out among his peers.

He had a healthy and balanced view of himself, life in general, and others, to be sure. But when he did wrong he owned up and learned from the consequences. He didn't mind chores or working with his daddy and he generally thought well of his siblings, though not without an occasional dispute. But he was over those kinds of things quickly.

And he cared to be reconciled with anyone he had a difference with. He was fascinated with the boy Jesus from his moma's bible stories and wondered if he might have something in common with Him. And it was that spiritually reflective side that caused him to stand out.

This reflective side was apparent in Joshua through the original stories that formed in his mind, and that he often shared. He enjoyed being alone for hours, exploring and processing his deep and insightful thoughts, or being on the fringes around others as an observer. After learning to write he eagerly began to harvest his creative thoughts onto paper. And his younger siblings enjoyed it when he would tell one of his stories, or read one to them.

Expansive young Joshua loved the sound of old New Orleans jazz. He sometimes sat and listened to the men as they interacted with their instruments through impromptu sessions. He was drawn to the free style of their unarranged sound as it alighted from the smooth blend of the pristine and rapid musical interaction that marvelously converged into the amazing stuff that was called 'jazz.' He equally enjoyed sitting and listening to the stories the old men told when they rested from the sessions.

He had an obvious ear for music. He could hear each of the distinct, different notes and chords within the music as they were being played and then step back and hear the entire sound of the music blending together. He could pick out the parts each musician played, sound them from his own mouth, each almost note-perfect, and teach them to someone else.

Joshua started a quartet as a young teen and taught the other guys their parts. The boys sang around the men of jazz on the street corner some evenings. He learned the banjo and often banged the keys on an old piano at Mingo's, the corner bar.

There Joshua would sit and teach himself to play. Occasionally, a jolly old musician, "Mr. Janks" gave him piano tips.

The Edwards family didn't look down on folk just because they drank. His daddy occasionally meandered down to Mingo's to have a social drink with some of the neighbors. But he never had more than a few. No one thought that Joseph Edwards would or could ever be found affected by alcohol. He didn't need that kind of a lift in life. He would tip a glass or two then excuse himself home to his family before the evening wore on.

Young Joshua was the kind of kid who cared about people, but not only for their physical needs. He also cared for their deeper side. And he cared about what was right and what was true. He cared that someone be whole in the spirit part of his or her life. His parents noticed this about him in his youth and encouraged him toward the pastorate.

But Joshua wasn't interested in employment in the formal arena of spiritual matters. He believed that he could more easily talk with others about spiritual life informally, through relationships and associations in the normal pathways of life.

And Joshua was not a stranger to tragedy. He didn't finish school and worked alongside his daddy until Joseph died in an accident when Joshua was engaged. He married in his early twenties and he and his wife had three children. His family was a special gift to him and he enjoyed them immensely. When he was thirty he lost his beloved wife to a mysterious virus. She was overcome with dehydration and went into a coma. By the time they could get her to the *Charity Hospital* downtown she was gone. Joshua was devastated.

He was left to raise his children as a single parent. And with the help of his moma and his siblings the children were cared for. More than once there were attempts to pair him with single women in the community. But Joshua was content and didn't pursue anything beyond friendships with any of them.

What he enjoyed was partaking in life with those in his community. Many of his peers and relatives stayed in the ninth ward. Quite a few of his elders were still alive in the community, including a few of the musicians, and Mingo.

His moma and a few of his aunts and uncles were still living.

By his fiftieth year Joshua was established as a well-respected and loved figure in his community. His children were grown. Two finished college and were young professionals. The other started his own contractor business after working with his daddy for ten years. All were out of the home.

Joshua lived alone, in the home he had built for his family, a modest three bedroom place with a front porch gallery and small yard. It was near his moma's place, two blocks from Mingo's. It had a large live-oak tree draped with *Spanish moss* in the back yard and a magnolia tree in the front.

He was asked to be an elder in the church body that he, his kids, and his ancestors were part of. But he graciously declined. Though Joshua was part of the life of those in the church his larger life was in the greater ninth ward community. He had a heart for those on the outside.

Some in the community attended different churches. Some didn't attend church at all. Of the latter many were considered 'outcasts' by some. But most of these people considered Joshua a friend and welcomed him into their often lonely lives.

To many in the community Joshua was a caring friend even though he stood for something that was set apart from the lives they were living. And the way he related to them broke down barriers. Often Joshua helped them repair their houses or boats. He could build or fix most anything and did so many times without charge.

The middle aged widower was often found sitting on an old box outside of Mingo's talking with the men. On occasion he'd have a drink with a few of the men inside. Always there was live interaction with occasional friendly arguing, good-natured ribbing, a tall tale or two, talk of current issues or days gone by, some unwholesome gossip or immoral jokes by the more unfettered, and stories passed along by the more poetic ones. And Joshua was one of the more poetic ones.

Once Upon A New Orleanian

He often invited friends to think about matters of the soul and of eternity, especially through his stories. Some talked behind his back or made fun of him. But Joshua took it in stride. And when he told stories they usually had a deeper meaning than the details of the story conveyed.

Over the years some found a new spiritual life through the storytelling and influence of Joshua.

Quite a few got involved with him in the church he attended and in several other churches in the community. They said that their lives had changed from being around Joshua. And they cherished him for it.

Joshua had a knack for telling stories and when he began one no one was surprised. Usually one of his stories came when he was serving someone, sitting around and talking about life or when others were in his company and had deferred to him on a topic. They were rarely forced. They came forth easily and fit the conversation like seasoned cloves of garlic and lemon in a mound of hot, freshly boiled crawfish.

One evening Joshua's children and grandchildren were at his place for supper. After some catching up, they asked him again why he told stories. Joshua said that he was in his element for a reason. He knew that many in the community were "like sheep without a shepherd" and that he cared for that to change.

"Most people's deepest needs aren't met by important people with titles or by a system."

He said. "For you and others like us the mysteries of the kingdoms' spiritual life are readily understood because we have humbled ourselves, embraced the truth and aren't seeking the wrong things. But to those who have not yet humbled themselves and come to the truth, and who are seeking the wrong things, I speak to them in story because their minds are closed to understanding the truth about themselves and God."

"If I speak to them in stories they have to think about what the meaning of the story is. This at least engages their thoughts more than if I told them a truth that I know they are currently closed to. Their attempt to catch the meaning of the story might whet their appetites for the truth inside it.

When they dismiss the truth that is directly given to them they have begun a habit of rejecting what is right. But if they dismiss the story that <u>contains</u> the truth after chewing on it for just a few minutes, then later, when they are alone, maybe they'll recall the flavor it gave them and chew on it some more.

Although some folk are hard-hearted and will never want to understand and always seek the wrong things, my stories have the effect of not letting them off the hook when it comes to giving an account of their lives. But for the others, and who knows who's who, I don't tell story's because I want to keep them confused and I DON'T want them to understand. I'm telling them stories because they are being confused by wanting something else and I DO want them to get beyond that and begin to seek true life and begin to understand."

"Like the one about the farmer and the seed?" His daughter said.

"Yes indeed!" He replied. "A farmer went out to throw the seed for planting," Joshua began. "Some of the seed landed on the road…"

The three young adult prodigy looked at one another and nodded in one accord. Their daddy had told and explained this one to them many times before.

Once Upon A New Orleanian

~

How would you explain
the man Joshua to a friend?

He is Far more caring
and personable
than you want Him to be,
while at the same time
more uncompromising
in morality and truth
than you suspect that He is.

~ Michael Joseph

Once Upon A New Orleanian

Once Upon A New Orleanian

Once Upon A New Orleanian

Once Upon A New Orleanian

Once Upon A New Orleanian

Once Upon A New Orleanian

Once Upon A New Orleanian

Once Upon A New Orleanian

www.ingramcontent.com/pod-product-compliance
Lightning Source LLC
Chambersburg PA
CBHW030120100526
44591CB00009B/477